ANIMALS
Doing Very Human Things
Coloring Book

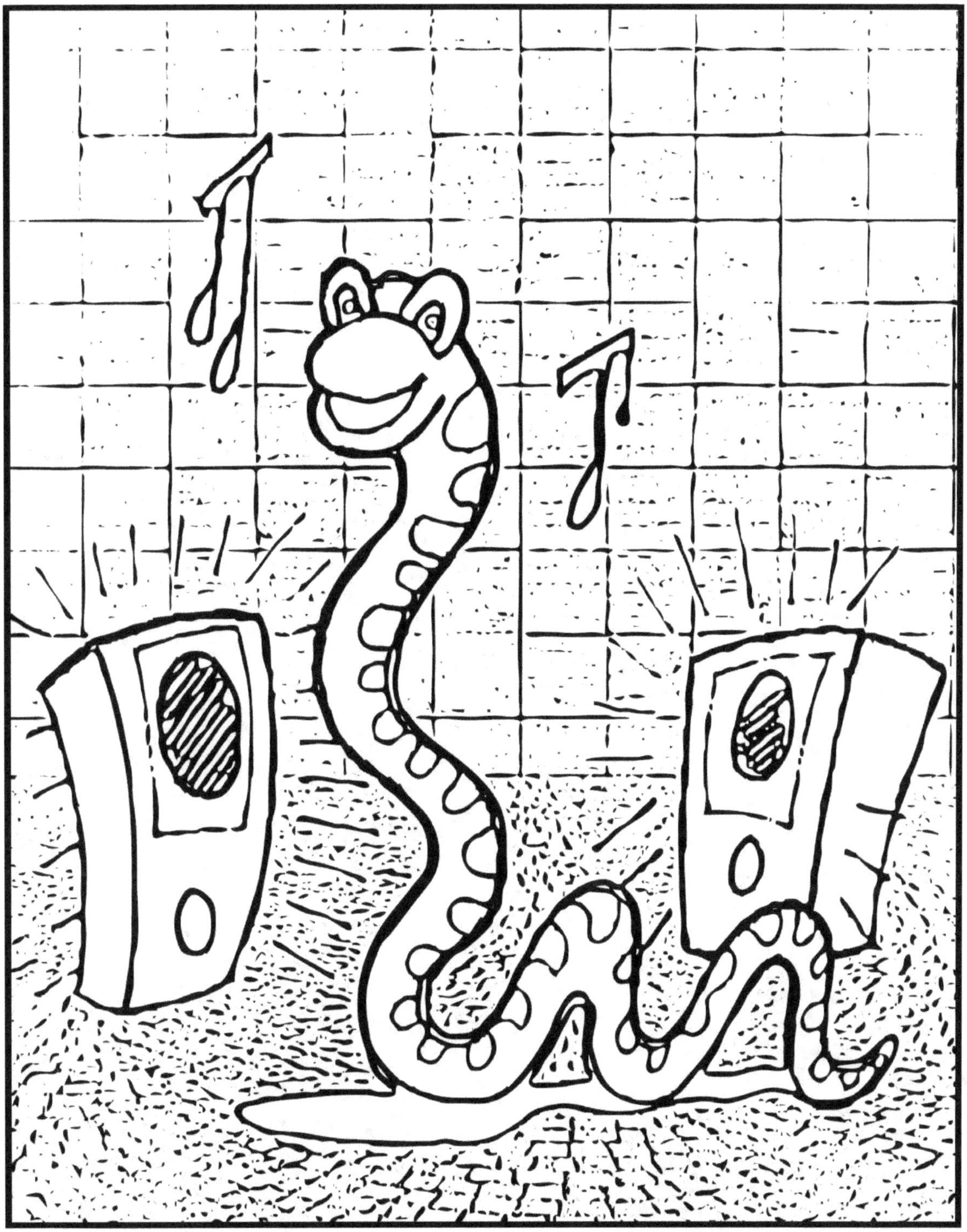

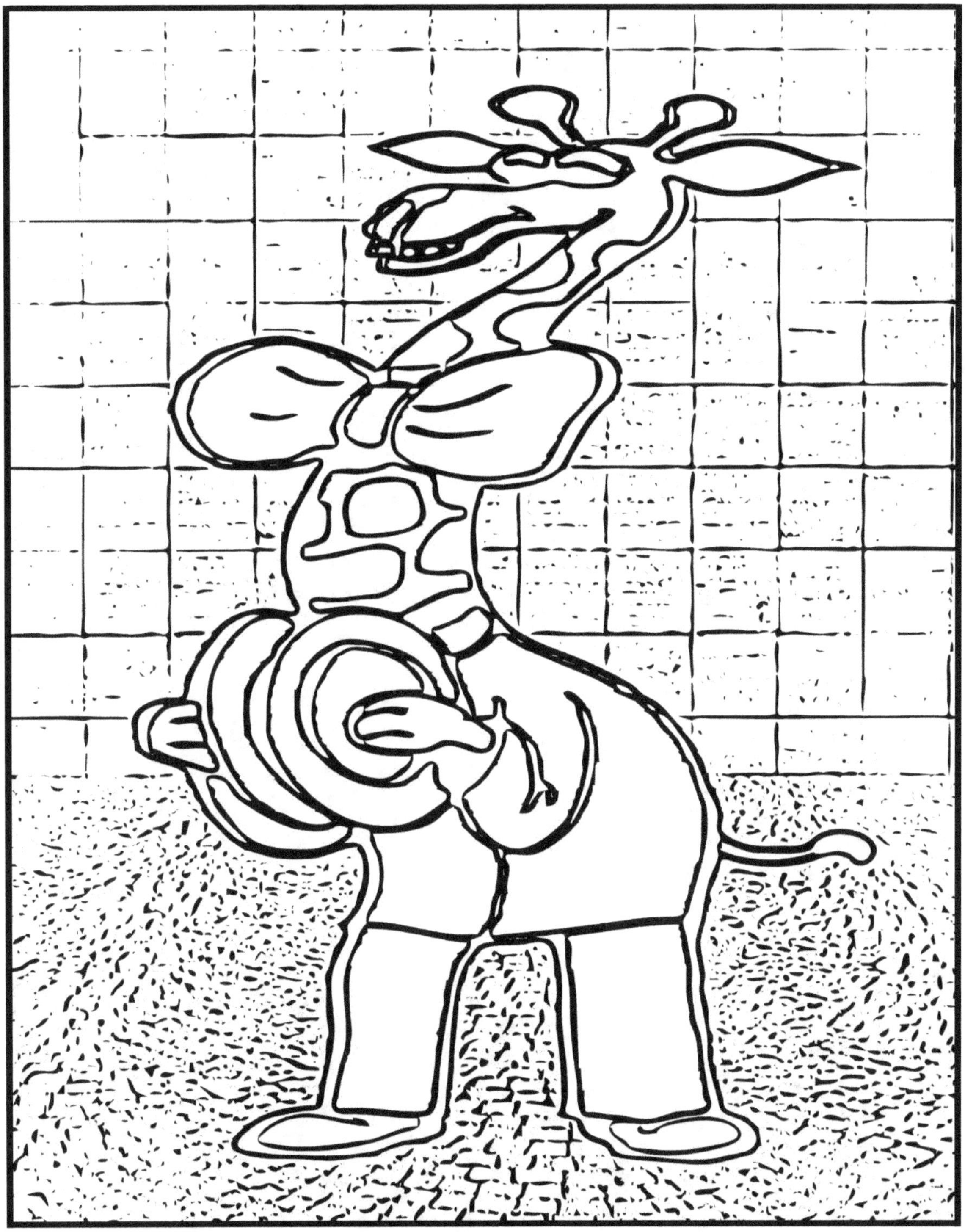

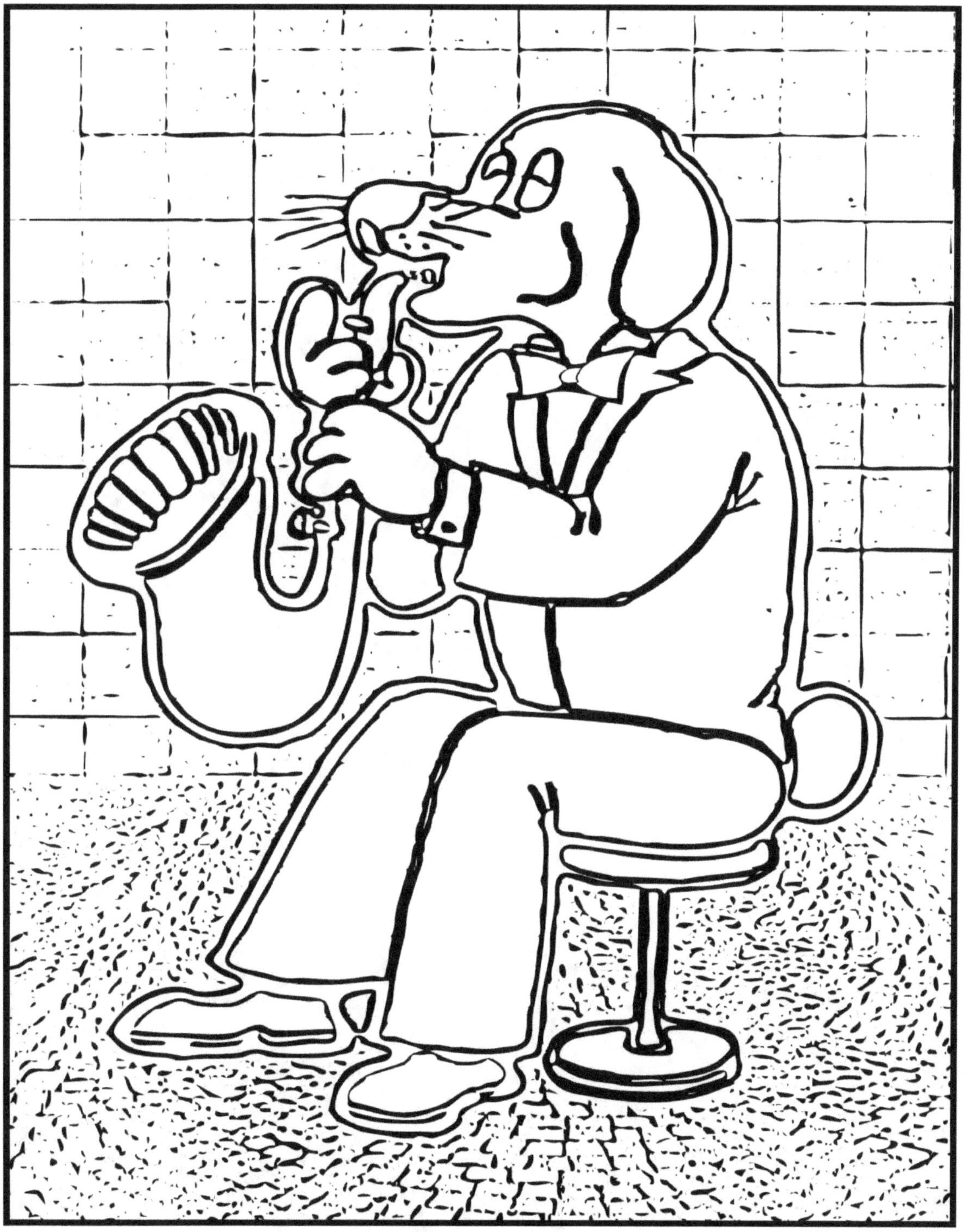

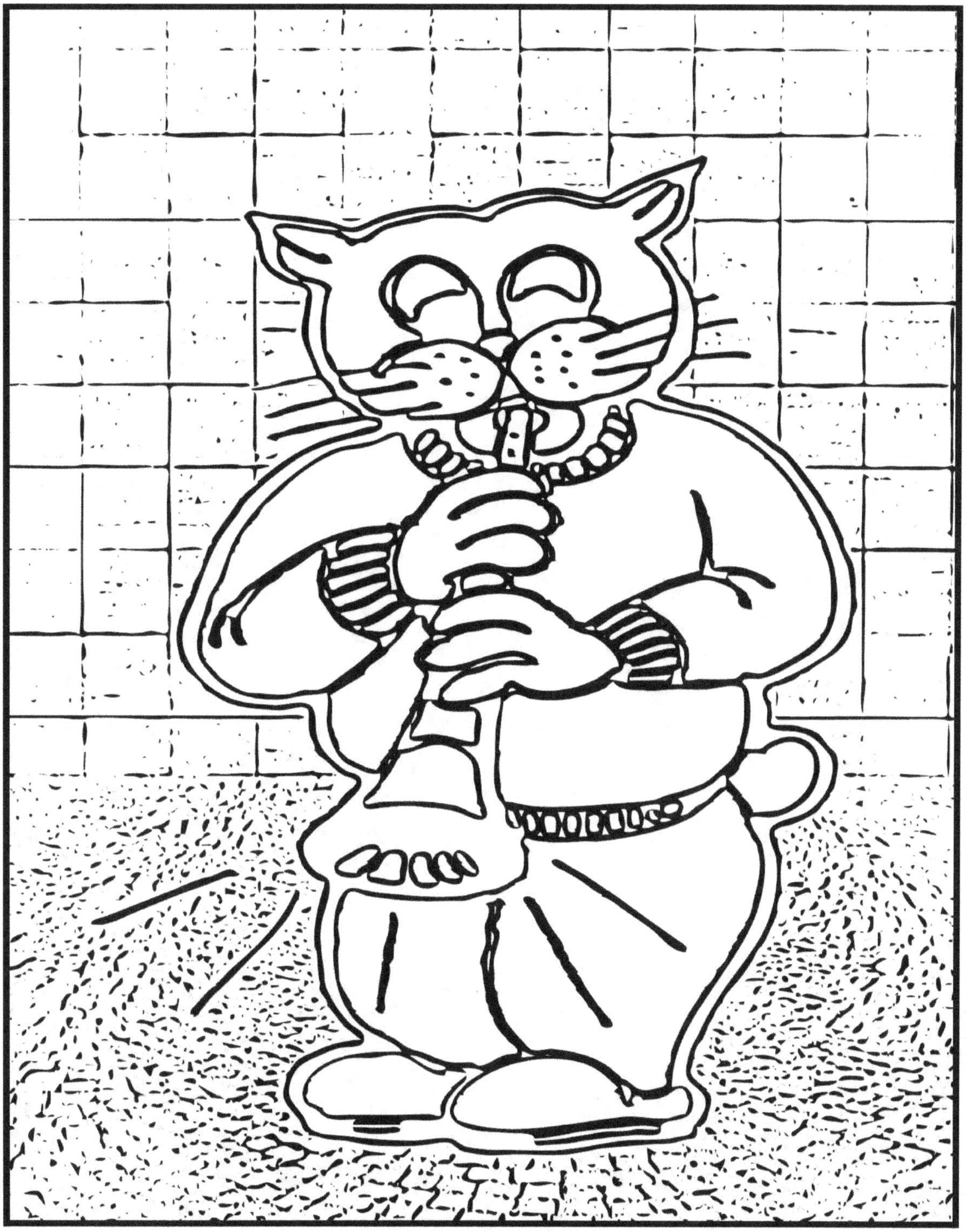

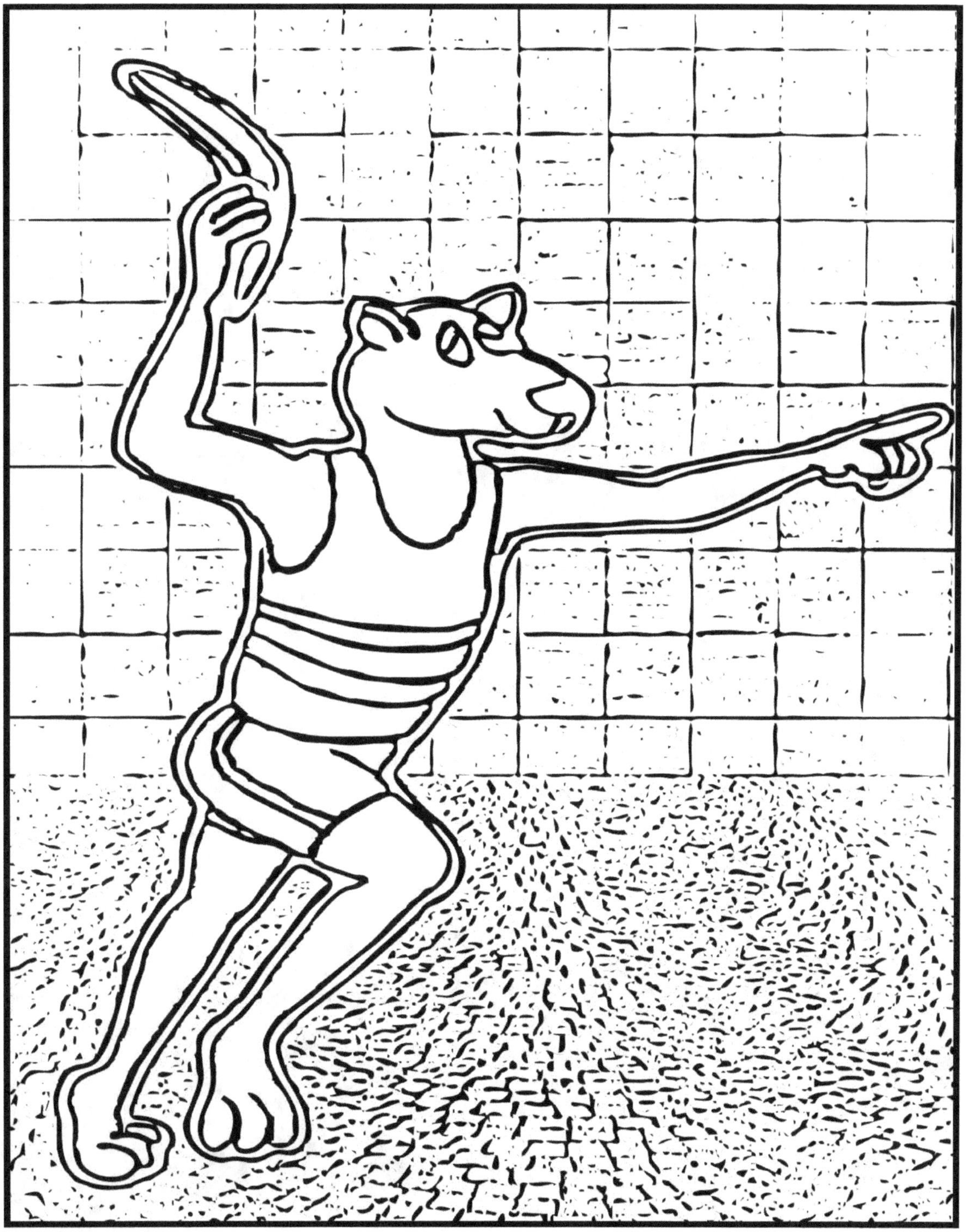

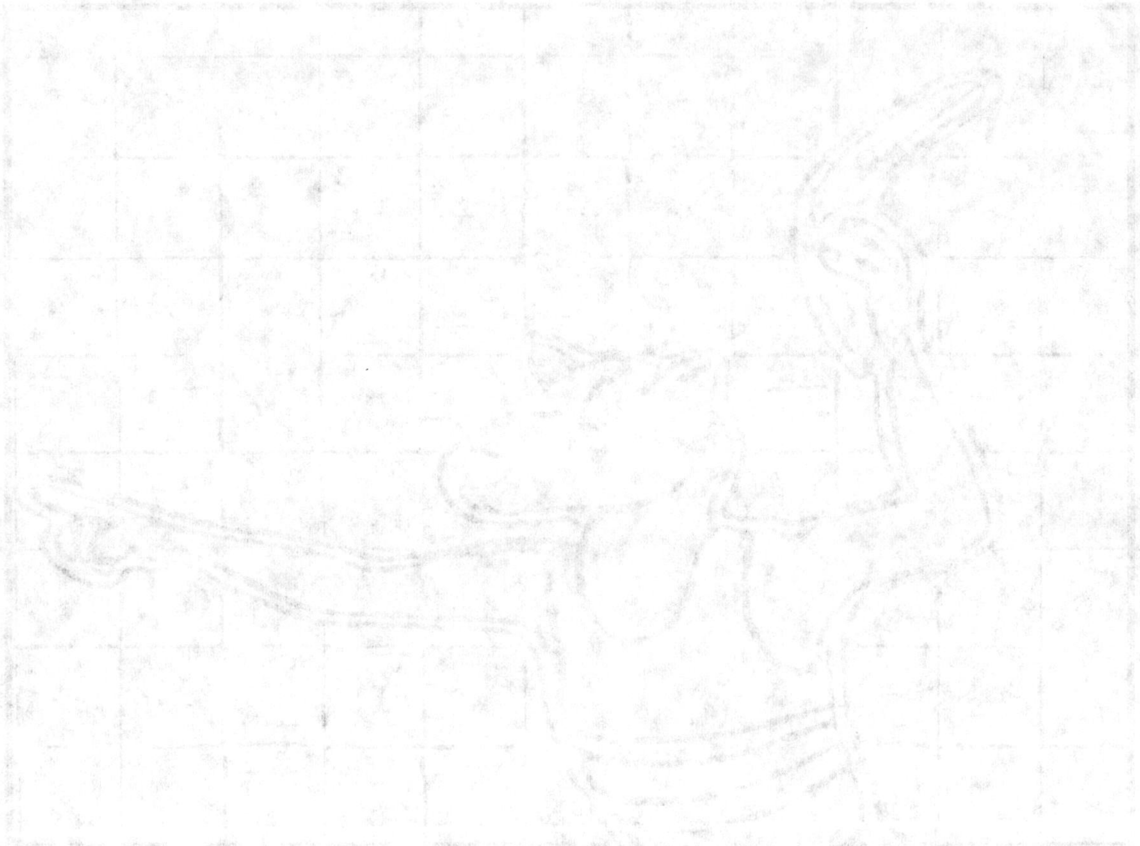

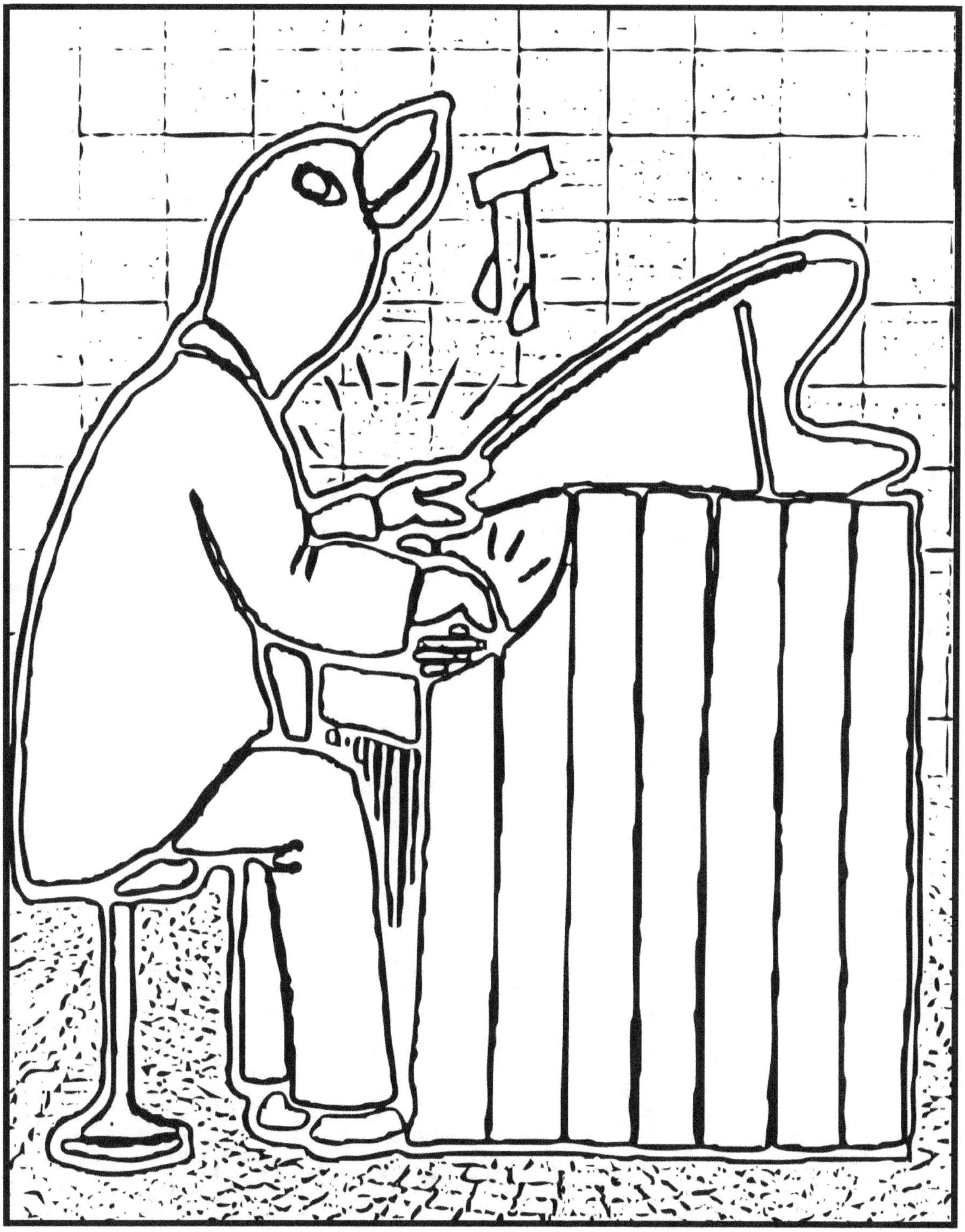

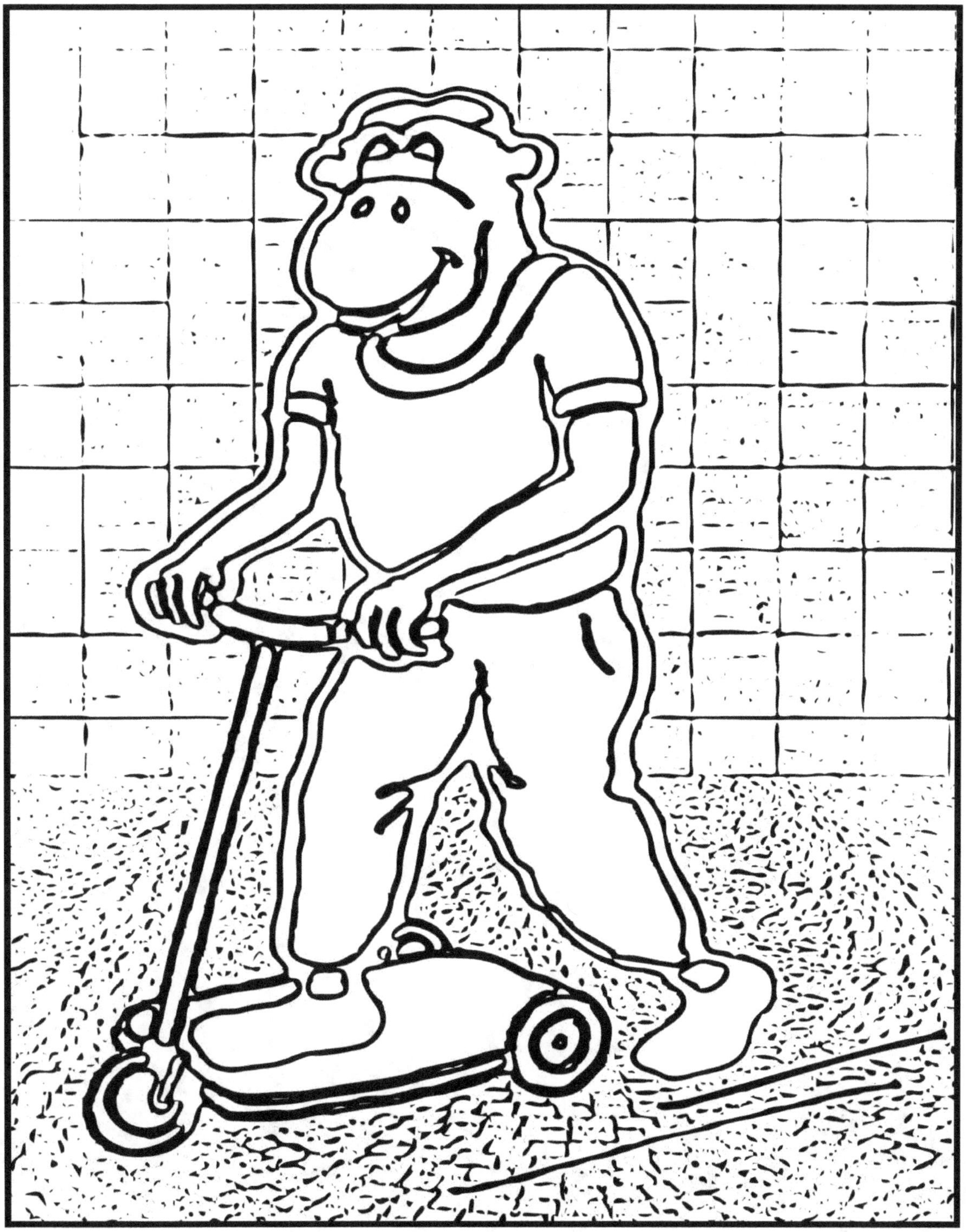

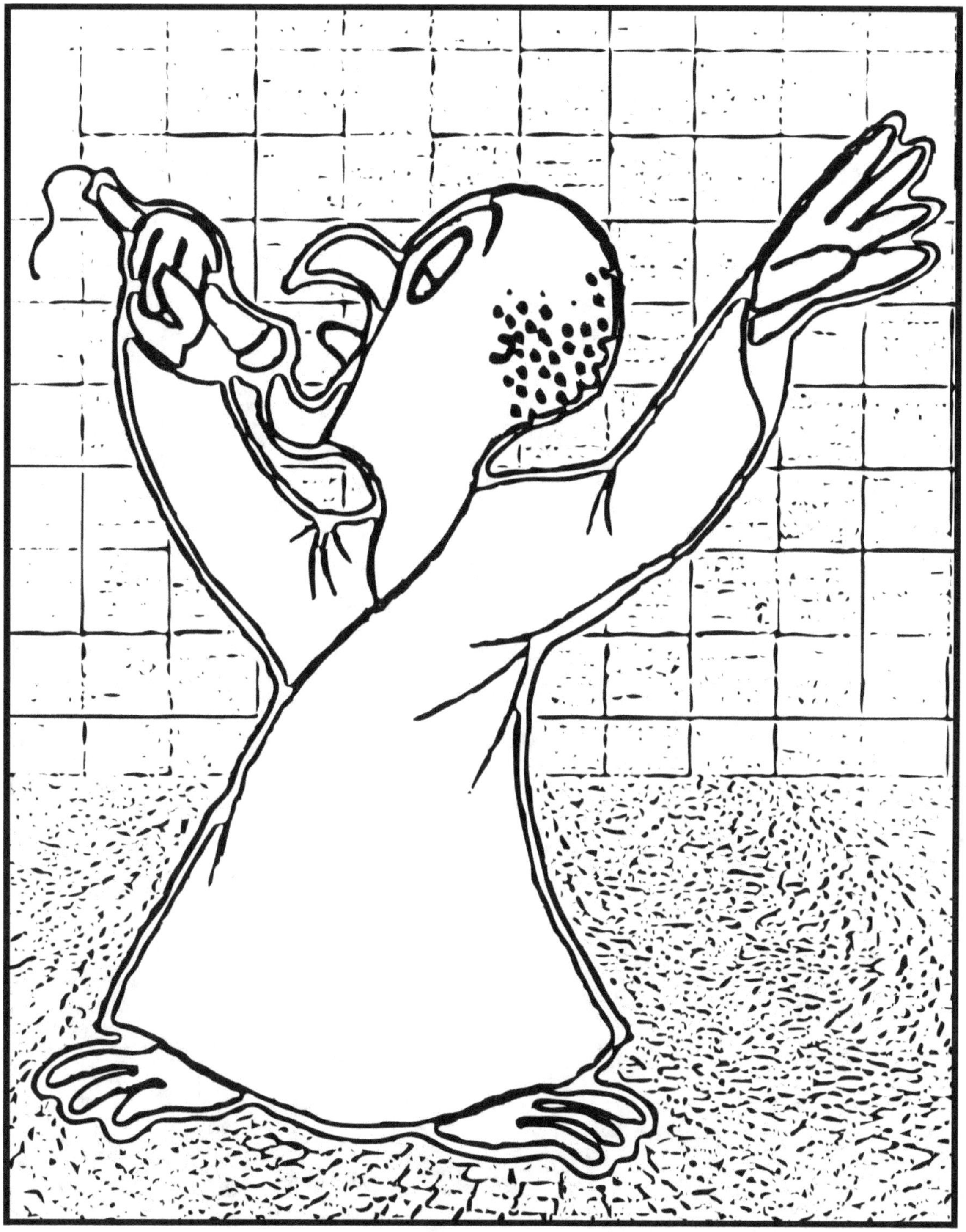

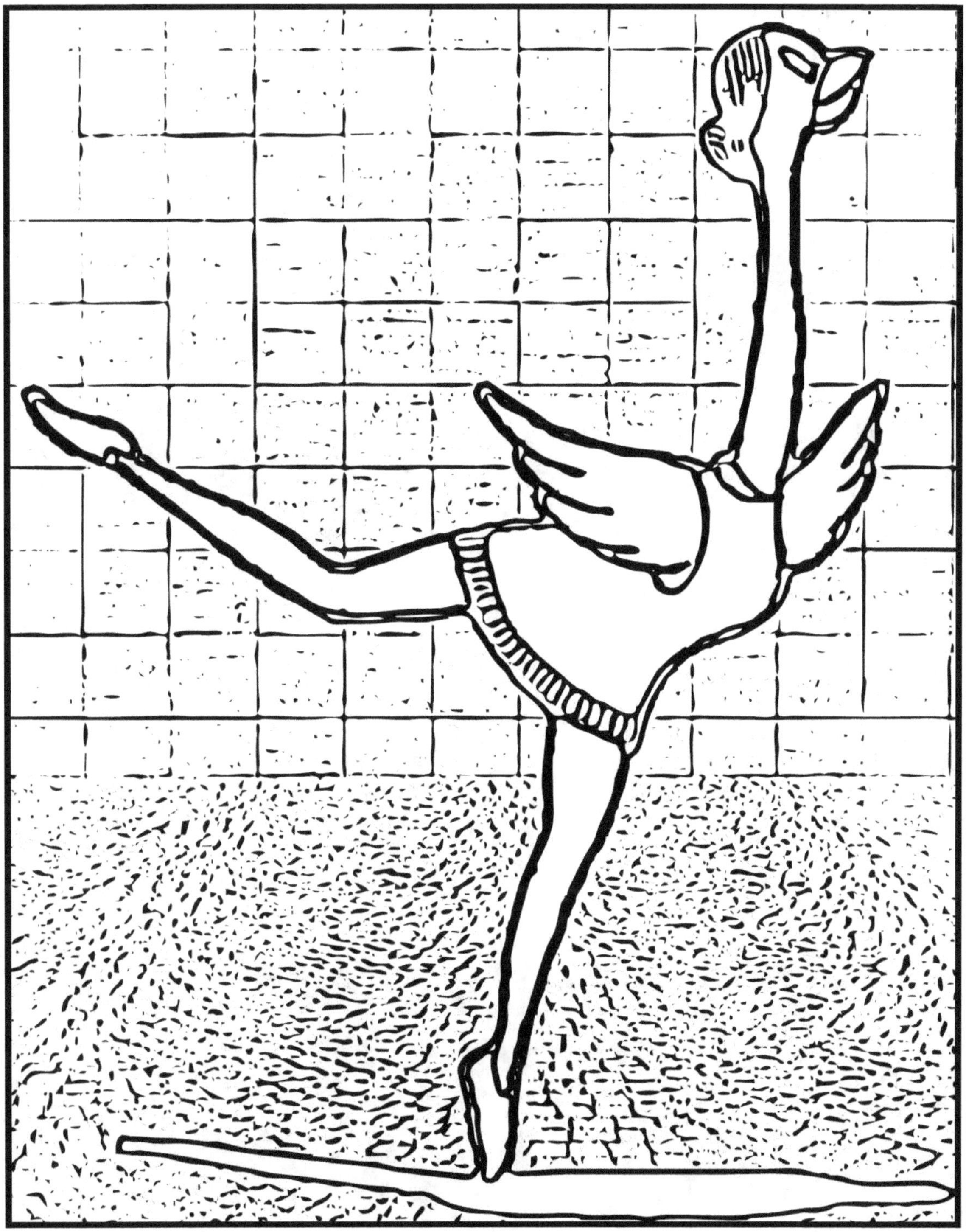

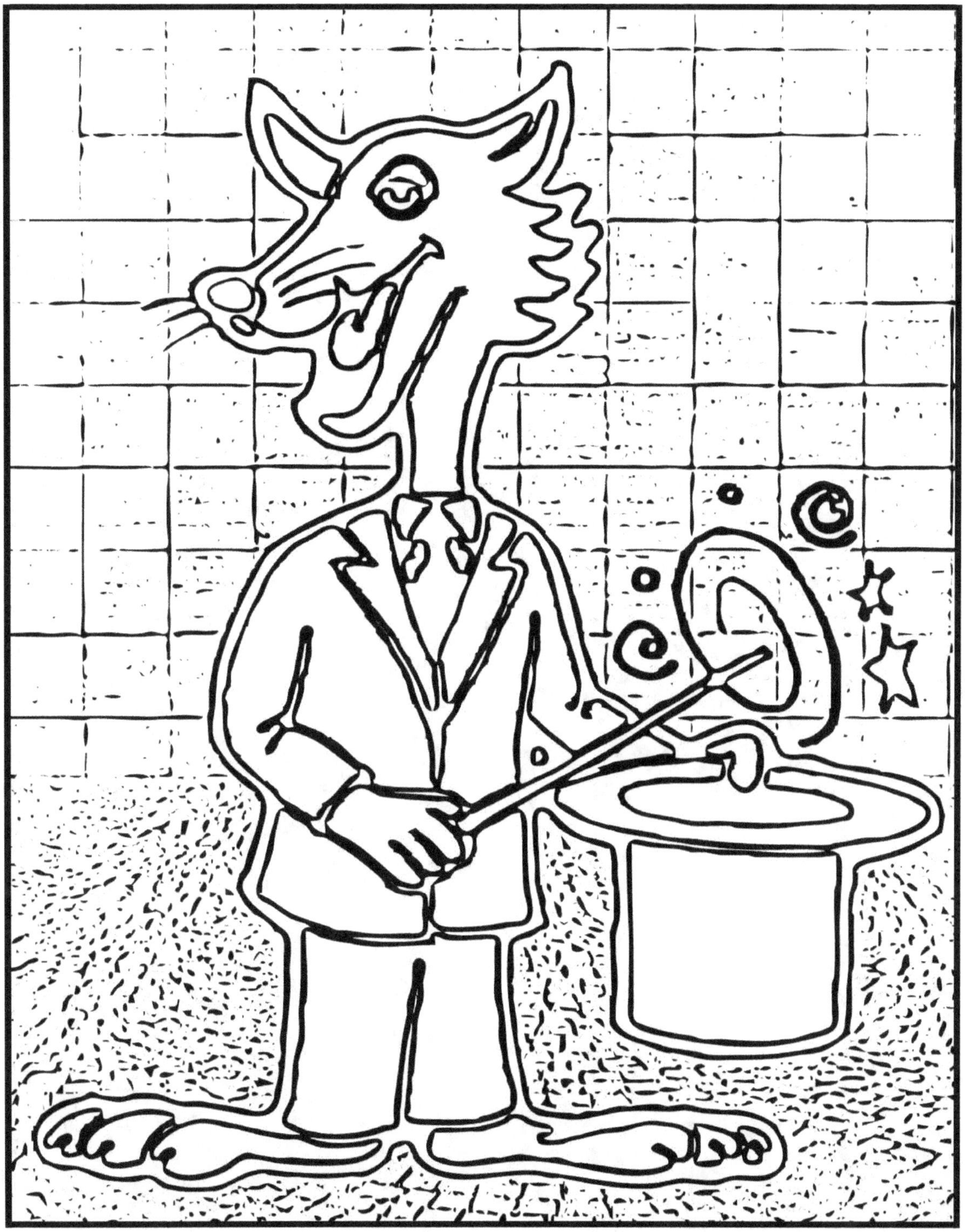

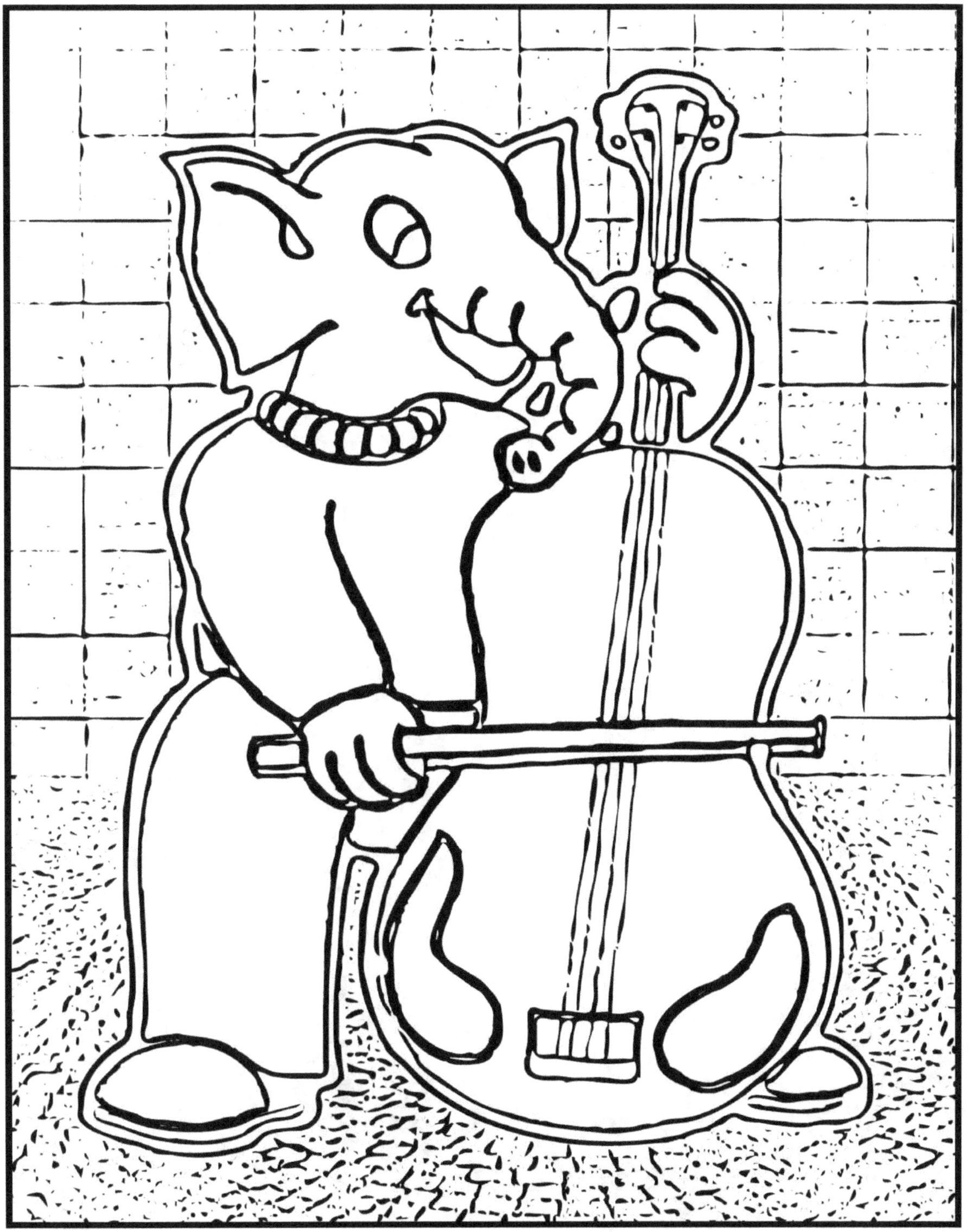

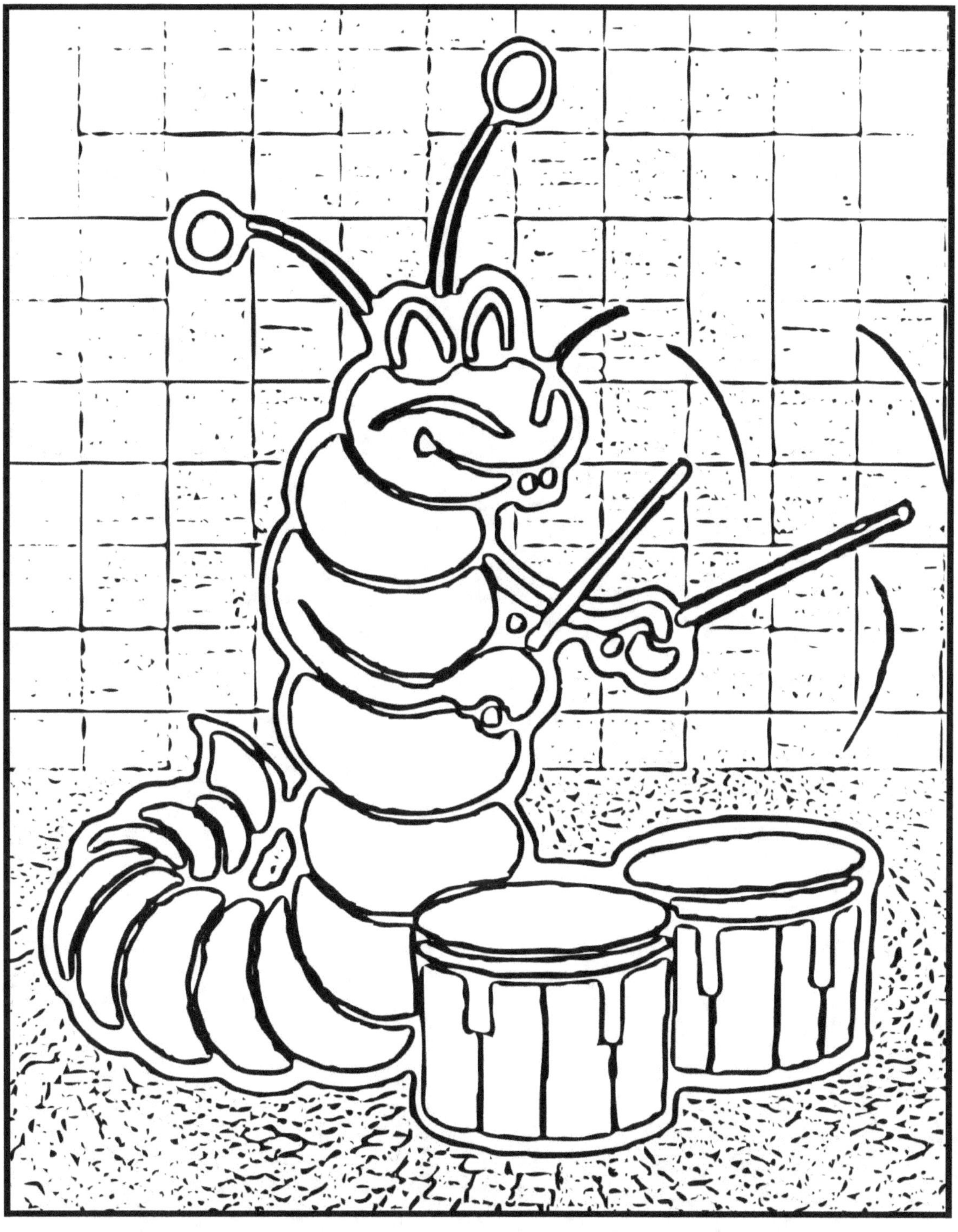

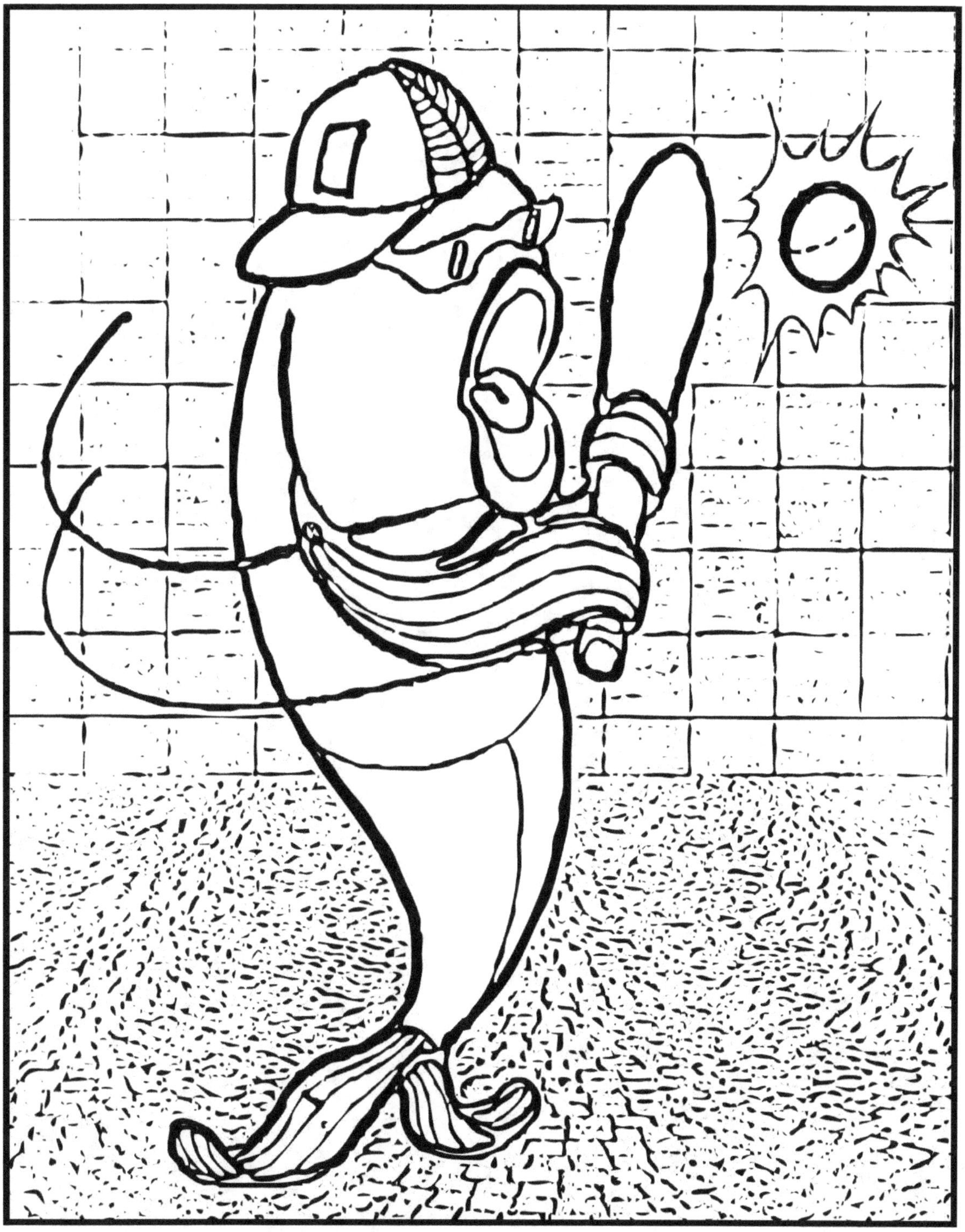

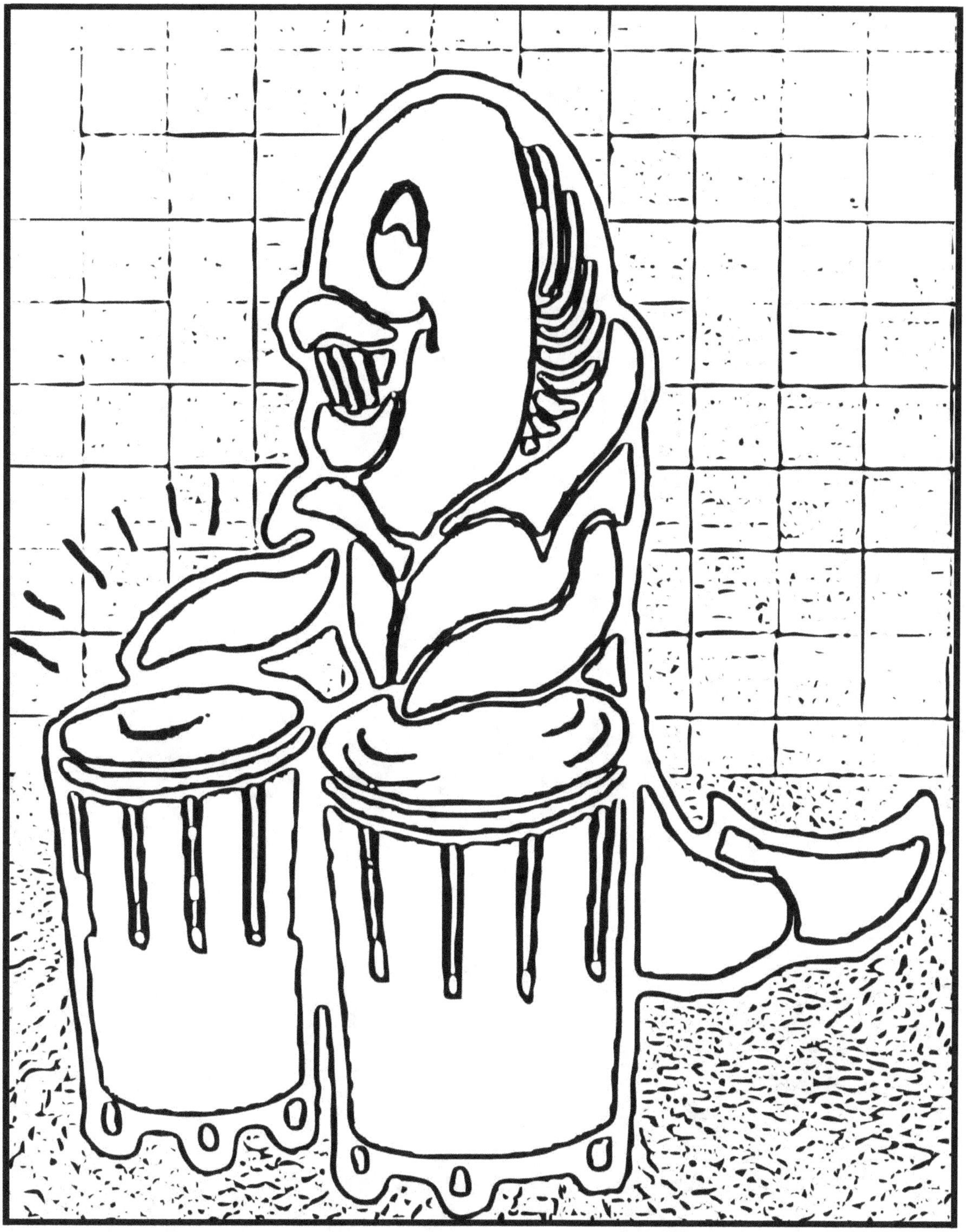

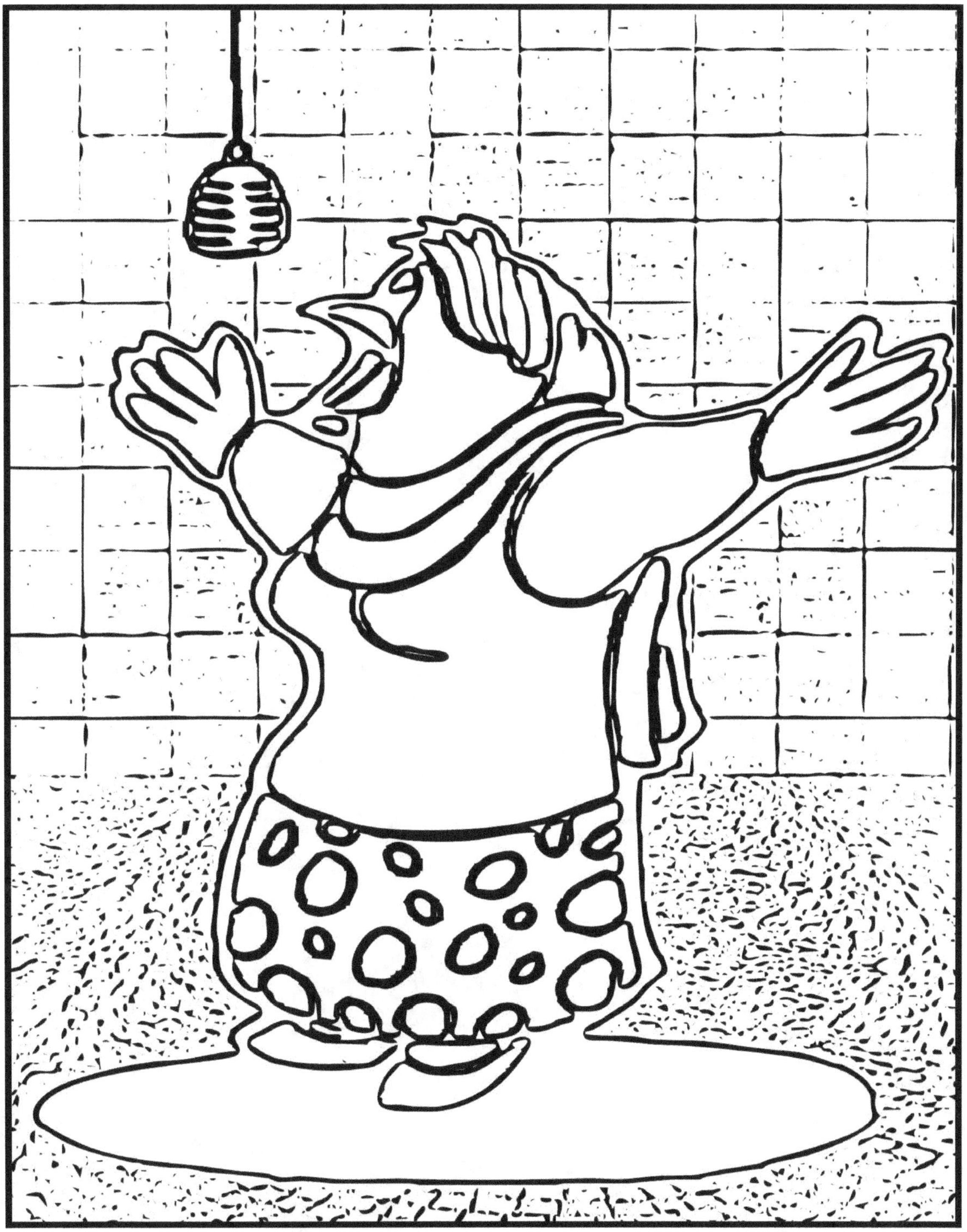

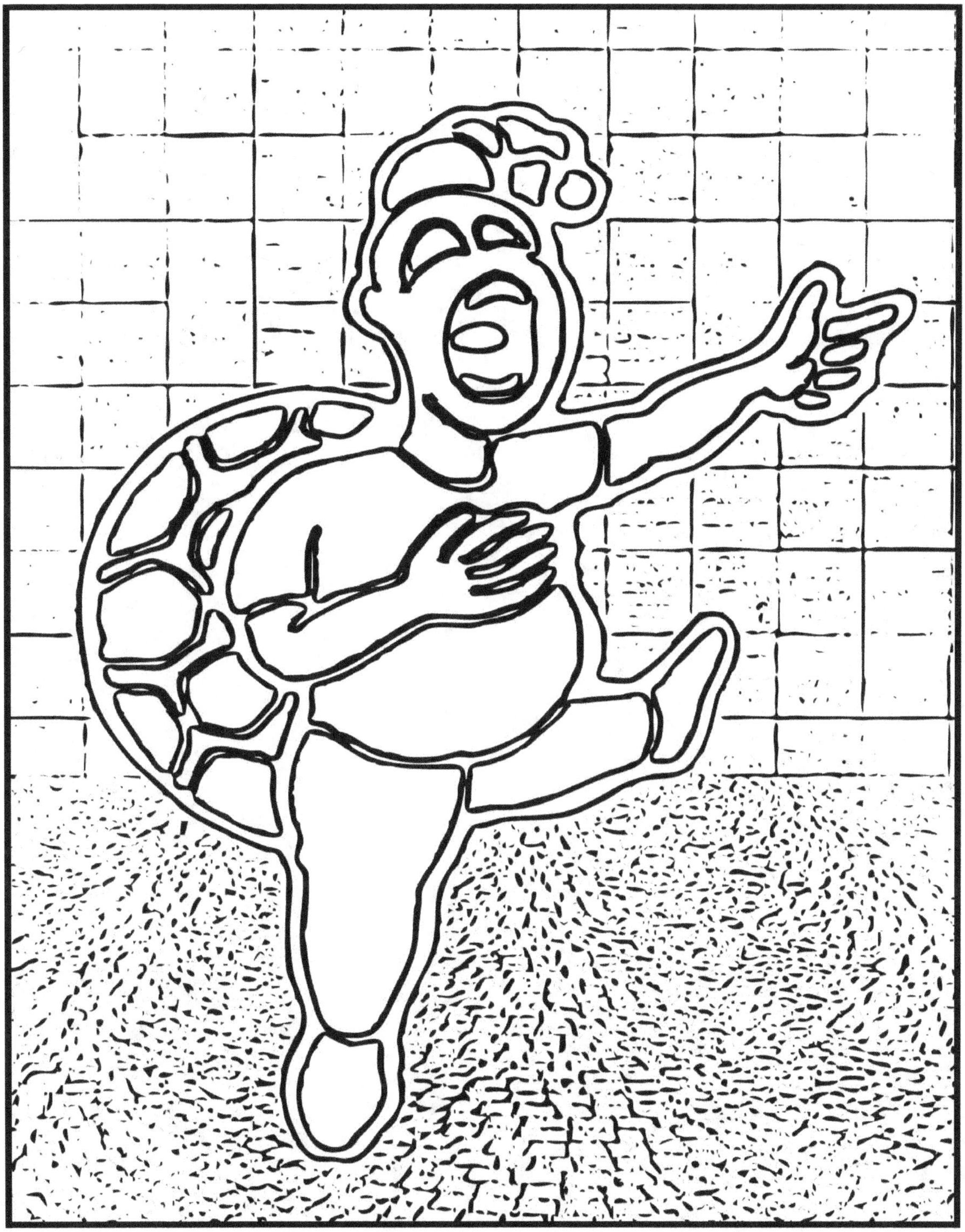

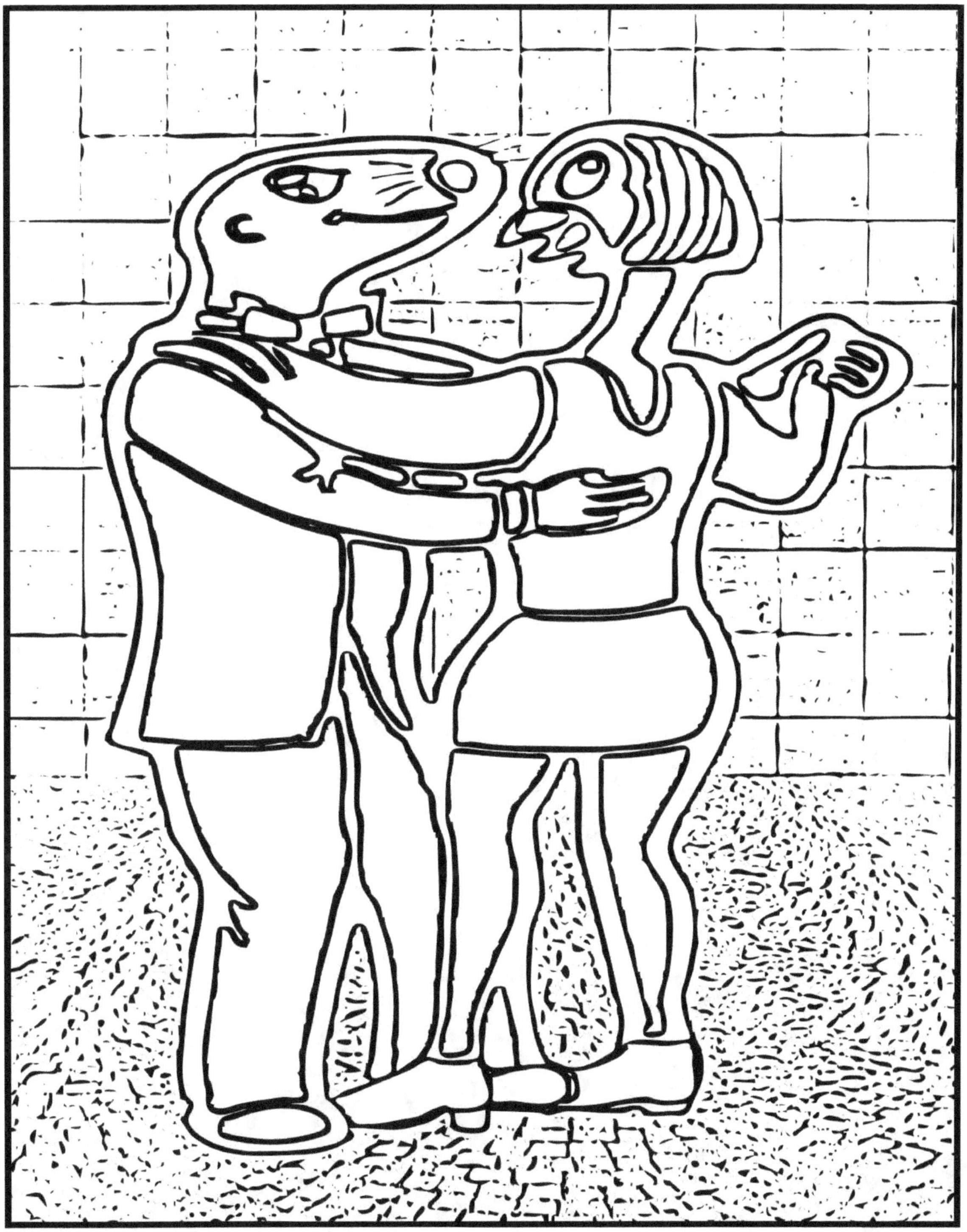

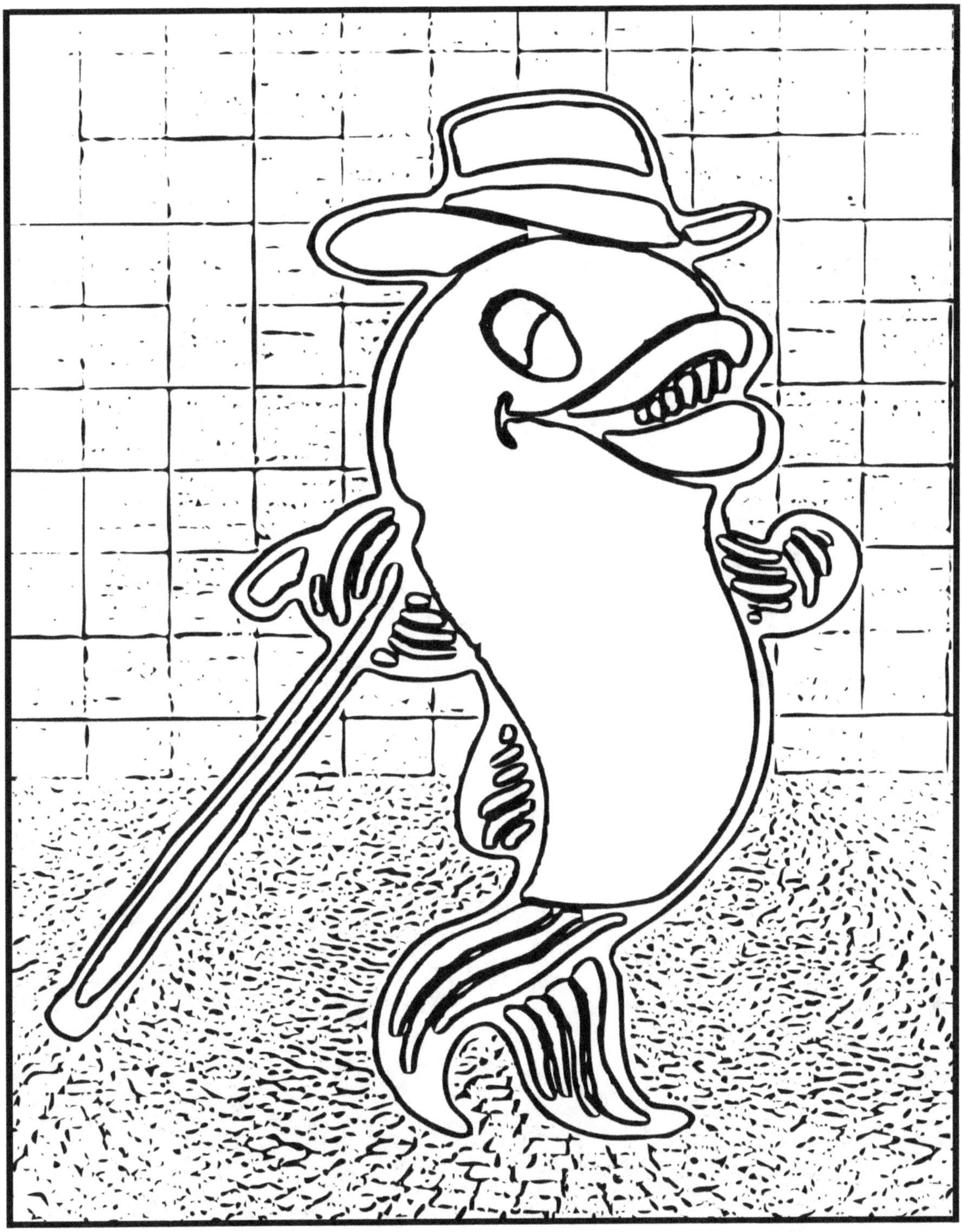

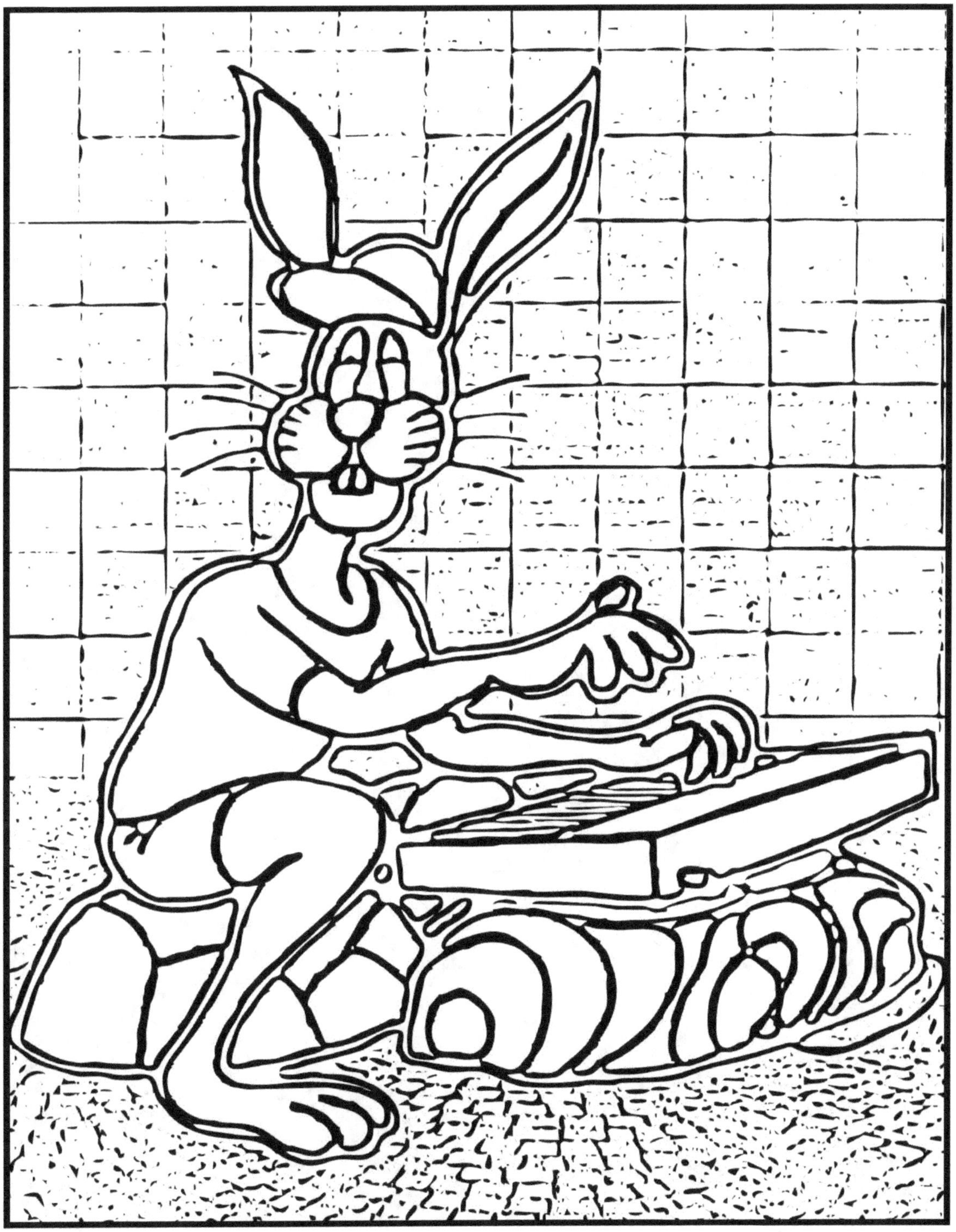

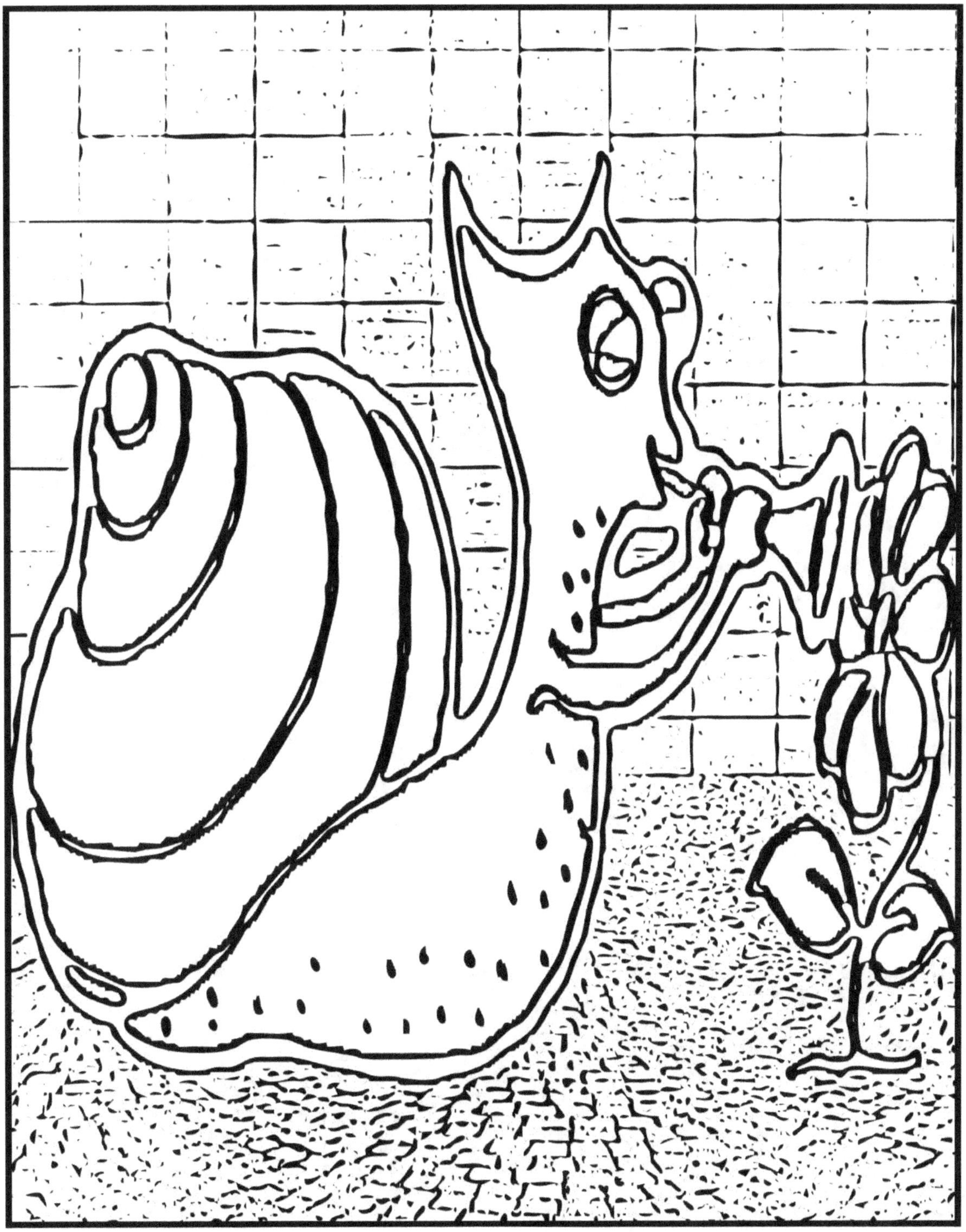

www.ingramcontent.com/pod-product-compliance
Lightning Source LLC
Chambersburg PA
CBHW081401170526
45166CB00010B/3158